Shake Hands With
LIFE

J. P. Vaswani

Sterling Paperbacks

Other Books By Dada J.P. Vaswani

In English:
10 Commandments of A Successful Marriage
108 Pearls of Practical Wisdom
108 Simple Prayers of A Simple Man
108 Thoughts on Success
114 Thoughts on Love
A Little Book of Life
A Treasure of Quotes
Around The Camp Fire
Begin The Day With God
Burn Anger Before Anger Burns You
Dada Answers
Daily Inspiration
Daily Inspiration (Booklet)
Destination Happiness
Dewdrops of Love
Does God Have Favourites?
Formula For Prosperity
Gateways to Heaven
God In Quest of Man
Good Parenting
What You Would Like To know About Hinduism
I am a Sindhi
In 2012 All Will Be Well
Joy Peace Pills
Kill Fear Before Fear Kills You
Ladder of Abhyasa
Lessons Life Has Taught Me
Life After Death
Management Moment by Moment
Mantras For Peace Of Mind
Many Paths: One Goal
Nearer, My God, To Thee!
New Education Can Make the World New
Peace or Perish
Positive Power of Thanksgiving
Sadhu Vaswani : His Life And Teachings
Saints For You and Me
Saints With A Difference
Secrets of Health And Happiness
Short Sketches of Saints Known & Unknown
Sketches of Saints Known & Unknown
Stop Complaining: Start Thanking!
Swallow Irritation Before Irritation Swallows You
Teachers are Sculptors
The Little Book of Freedom From Stress
The Little Book of Prayer
The Little Book of Service
The Little Book of Success
The Little Book of Wisdom
The Little Book of Yoga
The Magic of Forgiveness
The Perfect Relationship: Guru and Disciple
The Seven Commandments of the Bhagavad Gita
The Terror Within
The Way of Abhyasa (How To Meditate)
Thus Have I Been Taught
Tips For Teenagers
What You Would Like To know About Karma
Why Do Good People Suffer?
You Are Not Alone God Is With You!

Story Books:
101 Stories For You And Me
25 Stories For Children and also for Teens
Break The Habit
It's All A Matter of Attitude
More Snacks For The Soul
Snacks For The Soul
The Lord Provides
The Heart of a Mother
The King of Kings
The One Thing Needful
The Patience of Purna
The Power of Good Deeds
The Power of Thought
Trust Me All in All or Not at All
Whom Do You Love the Most
You Can Make A Difference

In Hindi:
Aalwar Santon Ki Mahan Gaathaayen
Atmik Jalpaan
Atmik Poshan
Bhakton Ki Uljhanon Kaa Saral Upaai
Bhale Logon Ke Saath Bura Kyon?
Brindavan Ka Balak
Dainik Prerna
Dar Se Mukti Paayen
Ishwar Tujhe Pranam
Jiski Jholi Mein Hain Pyaar
Krodh Ko Jalayen Swayam Ko Nahin
Laghu Kathayein
Mrutyu Hai Dwar… Phir Kya?
Nava Pushp (Bhajans In Hindi and Sindhi)
Prarthna ki Shakti
Pyar Ka Masiha
Sadhu Vaswani: Unkaa Jeevan Aur Shikshaayen
Safal Vivah Ke Dus Rahasya
Santon Ki Leela

In Sindhi:
Burn Anger Before Anger Burns You
Jaade Pireen Kaare Pandh
Munhjee Dil Te Lagee Laahootiyun Saan
Why Do Good People Suffer
Vatan Je Vannan De

In Marathi:
Krodhala Shaanth Kara, Krodhane Ghala Ghalnya Purvee (Burn Anger Before Anger Burns You)
Jiski Jholi Mein Hain Pyaar
Life After Death
Pilgrim of Love
Sind and the Sindhis
Sufi Sant (Sufi Saints of East and West)
What You Would Like To Know About Karma

In Kannada:
101 Stories For You And Me
Burn Anger Before Anger Burns You
Life After Death
Tips for Teenagers
Why do Good People Suffer

In Telugu:
Burn Anger Before Anger Burns You
Life after Death
What You Would Like To Know About Karma

In Arabic:
Daily Appointment With God
Daily Inspiration

In Chinese:
Daily Appointment With God

In Dutch:
Begin The Day With God

In Bahasa:
A Little Book of Success
A Little Book of Wisdom
Burn Anger Before Anger burns You
Life After Death

In Spanish:
Aprenda A Controlar Su Ira (Burn Anger Before Anger burns You)
Bocaditos Para el Alma (Snacks for the Soul)
Dios (Daily Meeting With God)
El Bein Quentu Hagas, Regresa (The Good You Do Returns)
Encontro Diario Com Deus (Daily Appontment With God)
Inicia Tu Dia Con Dios (Begin The Day With God)
L'Inspiration Quotidienne (Daily Inspiration)
Mas Bocaditos Para el Alma (More Snacks for the Soul)
Mata al miedo antes de que el miedo te mate (Kill Fear Before Fear Kills you)
Queme La Ira Antes Que La Ira Lo Queme A Usted(Burn Anger Before Anger Burns You)
Sita Diario ku Dios (I Luv U, God!)
Todo es Cuestion de Actitud! (Its All A Matter of Attitude)
Vida despu'es de la Muerte (Life After Death)

In Gujrati:
Its All A Matter of Attitude

In Oriya:
Burn Anger Before Anger burns You
More Snacks For the Soul
Pilgrim of Love
Snacks For The Soul
Why Do Good People Suffer

In Russian:
What would you like to Know about Karma

In Tamil:
10 Commandments of a Successful Marriage
Burn Anger Before Anger burns You
Daily Appointment with God
Its All a Matter of Attitude
Kill Fear Before Fear Kills You
More Snacks For the Soul
Secrets of Health and Happiness
Snacks For The Soul
Why Do Good People Suffer

In Latvian:
The Magic of Forgiveness

Other Publications:

Recipe Books:
90 Vegetarian Sindhi Recipes
Di-li-cious Vegetarian Recipes
Simply Vegetarian

Books on Dada J. P. Vaswani:
A Pilgrim of Love
Dada J.P. Vaswani: His Life and Teachings
Dada J.P. Vaswani's Historic Visit to Sind
Dost Thou Keep Memory
How To Embrace Pain
Living Legend
Moments with a Master

STERLING PAPERBACKS
An imprint of
Sterling Publishers (P) Ltd.
A-59, Okhla Industrial Area, Phase-II, New Delhi-110020.
Tel: 26387070, 26386209; Fax: 91-11-26383788
E-mail: mail@sterlingpublishers.com
www.sterlingpublishers.com

Shake Hands With Life
© 2011, J. P. Vaswani
ISBN 978 81 207 5343 3

All rights are reserved.
No part of this publication may be reproduced, stored in a retrieval system or transmitted, in any form or by any means, mechanical, photocopying, recording or otherwise, without prior written permission of the author.

DADA VASWANI BOOKS
Visit us online to purchase books on self improvement, spiritual advancement, meditation and philosophy. Plus audio cassettes, CDs, DVDs, monthly journals and books in Hindi.
www.dadavaswanisbooks.org

Printed in India
Printed and Published by Sterling Publishers Pvt. Ltd., New Delhi-110 020.

Contents

Chapter 1
Life is Rocking! — 7

Chapter 2
Life is the Greatest Gift! — 11

Chapter 3
We're All in it Together! — 17

Chapter 4
Why Do We Undervalue Life? — 25

Chapter 5
Overcoming Depression — 35

Chapter 6
Suicide is Not A Solution! — 41

Chapter 7
Practical Suggestions — 47

Chapter 8
A Simple Meditation to Build Positive Thinking and Self Esteem — 75

CHAPTER 1

LIFE IS ROCKING!

If I were to ask you what is the most beautiful thing in your life, what would your answer be? Let me guess:

- Friendship
- Love
- Laughter
- Family
- Books
- Music
- Knowledge and Learning
- Nature
- Fresh air and Open spaces...

The list would be endless, would it not? It would vary from individual to individual. Your list would be quite different from mine, and your friend's or your brother's, wouldn't it?

This only shows that the magnificent kaleidoscope of life is made up of innumerable, beautiful, valuable facets. The glory and wonder, the joy and laughter, the munificence and colour of life are amazing and awe inspiring.

Yes, indeed, the blessings of life are many. But I am sure that you would agree with me that the supreme gift each one of us has received is life itself. The love and support of our family; the laughter and companionship we share with our friends; the beauty and serenity of nature – the blue skies, the chirping of birds, the swaying green grass, the gentle breeze...

Can you see a baby gurgling and babbling its thoughts aloud, and walk away indifferently?

Can you watch the magnificent red, orange and russet shades of the sunset and simply close your eyes and mind?

Can you behold a bud unfurling its petals into full bloom and not be awed by its life and beauty?

God, who gave us this human body, endowed us with the five senses so that we could appreciate the magnificence and grandeur of the infinite Universe which is so perfect and well planned.

And the most beautiful thing about this Divine Plan is that He made *you* a vibrant part of it!

The most beautiful thing about life is that *you* are alive!

So let us make the most of every moment, every breath of this beautiful life!

What are you waiting for? Life is calling out to you to take it on, and make the most of it. Only a weakling would decline such an offer. Never turn your back on life. Life is meant to be lived!

Take to your heart the sheer joy and beauty that is life!

Life is rocking! You only need to have the right attitude!

> GOD GAVE US THE GIFT OF LIFE; IT IS UPTO US TO GIVE OURSELVES THE GIFT OF LIVING WELL!
>
> VOLTAIRE

CHAPTER 2

LIFE IS THE GREATEST GIFT!

Human life is a rare and precious gift from God. We should live this life in such a way that our body and mind are cultivated in the best possible manner; that right thoughts may come to us, right words are spoken by us, right actions are performed, and right results are obtained, all leading to the ultimate goal – liberation!

All religions constantly remind us how rare it is to find ourselves in human form on earth. We should feel enormous appreciation for being here as individual spirits filled with consciousness – whether we are drinking water or chopping wood, sowing seeds or writing programmes, studying or teaching, reading or reflecting, working or keeping a home.

Every seed that sprouts is a miracle of nature.

How much more miraculous is the human birth, so generously bestowed upon us by God!

How fortunate are we to receive this precious, priceless gift of the human birth!

Once, I saw a six year old throwing a tantrum. It was his birthday, and he had got several gifts from his family and friends. But the moment his mother told him to switch off the TV and go to bed, he began to sulk and complain. Gently she reminded him that obedience and good behaviour was the least she could expect from him after the veritable shower of gifts he had received. You should have seen and heard his response!

"I didn't ask you for a bicycle! I don't want a computer game! Who wants to play cricket anyway? You can keep all your gifts because I don't want them!"

I do hope you are not in the least like this ungrateful child.

Can you imagine how his mother must have felt at such an outburst? I don't know, but some mothers have a marvellous sense of humour. Let's hope that she just laughed it off!

But I do know some people who say to God, "I did not ask to be born in this world. Why did

You make me? You can keep this life with You – I did not want it in the first place!"

Now that is not just ingratitude and bad temper – it is stupidity and insensitivity.

There is an old Indian proverb: you need a wall to splash the paint on.

What would you do with paints and colours if you didn't have a surface to paint on? Your life is the wall, the blank slate, the *kora kagaz* on which you can paint any picture of your choice.

Life is the greatest gift that God has conferred upon you. You cannot – must not be ungracious about it.

It's easy to be grateful to God when the going is easy: but may I say to you, you must be grateful to Him even when the going is tough. You may be suffering; you may be facing obstacles; you may be stumbling at every step; but you are still alive – and while there is life, there is hope!

Just think – you may have been a mushroom or a weed; an insect or a worm; a snake or a scorpion; a dog or a cat – but God made you a human being – the crown of His Creation. And you can think; you can reason; you can reflect; you can laugh and cry!

Social scientists often say that man is a political animal – or a party animal; but I think the best thing about the human species is that we are thinking, talking, laughing animals.

We are different from the rest of creation: we are the best, because God endowed us with those special gifts!

> I LIKE LIVING. I HAVE SOMETIMES BEEN WILDLY, DESPAIRINGLY, ACUTELY MISERABLE, RACKED WITH SORROW, BUT THROUGH IT ALL I STILL KNOW QUITE CERTAINLY THAT JUST TO BE ALIVE IS A GRAND THING.
>
> AGATHA CHRISTIE

Each one of us is unique and precious, and each one has been allocated their special purpose in life. It is up to us to discover and fulfill it.

To breathe, to live, to think, to laugh, to feel – believe me friends, these are faculties that you cannot buy with money.

And yet they are yours – for free!

You have received the miraculous gift of human life – when will you have such an opportunity again? Give yourself the gift of living life to the fullest!

Maximise Your Life!

- Change your attitude: renew your perspective.
- Change your thinking – transform your life.
- Take time to relax – refresh your spirit.
- Live in the present.
- Appreciate this moment.
- Cultivate loving awareness.
- Remember, you have the innate ability to reinvent your life.
- Be grateful for the simple gifts of God that are all around you.
- Make each moment count.
- Realise the power of life and the presence of God in your life.

CHAPTER 3

We're All in It Together!

What I would like to talk to you about now is this wonderful phenomenon called the interconnectedness of life – the interdependence of all creation. Sounds very difficult when I say it – but it is all so utterly and beautifully simple. That's why I chose that line from the song which we have all heard as children:

We're all in it together!

The poet John Donne put it so aptly when he wrote: *No man is an island.*

By myself, I am not complete, sufficient or whole. What makes me unique, what makes me special, are my links to other human beings.

And they are very many: my parents who brought me into this world, took care of me when I was helpless and incapable of taking care of myself. My family and friends who are always there for me, and ever ready to share my joys and sorrows; my teachers, elders and preceptors who have freely bestowed their time and effort to teach me, guide me and show me the right way...

And this list will only grow, as you grow older. Some of you may leave home to pursue higher studies. Some of you go to far away cities and countries to pursue a promising career. Some of you may get married and settle down to life in a completely new setting – and what wonderful new horizons open up before you!

Life is interconnected. We are all linked to each other by an invisible silken cord that binds us together as children of God, children of Mother Earth and inheritors of all the wealth of this Universe.

This is a Cosmic Link which I must never break.

And how intimately our life is bound with nature and the seasons! How effortlessly we adapt to summer and winter, sunshine and rain, mist and fog, day and night, heat and cold!

As human beings, we need food. How many of us grow our own food? Our brothers, the farmers grow food for us. How many of us *cook* our own food? Even more people are linked with us. What would we do without them? Where would we be without them?

Have you heard this joke about the young man who went to the railway track to end his life? He packed a bag of sandwiches to take with him. When someone pointed out that he was going to die – and not leaving for a picnic or a day's work – he solemnly pointed out that the train might be late and he did not want to 'go' hungry!

Not only do we need food; we also need clothes, shelter. We need an education; we need a job; we need friends and neighbours; we need shopkeepers and others who provide us essential services.

If you ask me, I will add: I need books and writing materials, which are almost as important for me as food and water.

If I ask you, you who are members of the younger generation, you will say to me that you need your cell phones, your computers, your MP3 players and your iPods, for you cannot imagine life without these gadgets.

Dear friends, there is not a living soul on earth that does not want to be happy. Everyone wants to be happy. But happiness is interconnected.

People need other people; people need each other.

You are never alone! You did not come into this world to live in isolation, like one of those unicellular organisms!

> I THINK WHAT MAKES US HUMAN — IS OUR INTERCONNECTEDNESS WITH PEOPLE. IT'S OUR ABILITY TO FORM AND MAINTAIN RELATIONSHIPS. IT'S THE BAROMETER BY WHICH WE CALL OURSELVES HUMAN.
>
> THOMAS JANE

When you realise the interconnectedness of all life, you will also realise that you are linked in one way or another to everything else upon this earth.

In a sense, your life is not your own!

When you begin to appreciate human interdependence, you will never ever harm another creature, nor ever harm yourself!

May I share with you this beautiful declaration written by five members of the David Suzuki Foundation team in 1992, for the United Nations' Earth Summit in Rio de Janeiro? In 2001, Finnish composer Pehr Henrik Nordgren wrote his Symphony no. 6 – "Interdependence" based on this declaration.

Declaration of Interdependence between Humans and the Natural World

This We Know
We are the earth, through the plants and animals that nourish us.
We are the rains and the oceans that flow through our veins.

We are the breath of the forests of the land, and the plants of the sea.
We are human animals, related to all other life as descendants of the firstborn cell.
We share with these kin a common history, written in our genes.
We share a common present, filled with uncertainty.
And we share a common future, as yet untold.
We humans are but one of thirty million species weaving the thin layer of life enveloping the world. The stability of communities of living things depends upon this diversity.
Linked in that web, we are interconnected — using, cleansing, sharing and replenishing the fundamental elements of life.
Our home, planet Earth, is finite; all life shares its resources and the energy from the sun, and therefore has limits to growth.
For the first time, we have touched those limits.
When we compromise the air, the water, the soil and the variety of life, we steal from the endless future to serve the fleeting present.

This We Believe

Humans have become so numerous and our tools so powerful that we have driven fellow creatures to extinction, dammed the great rivers, torn down ancient forests, poisoned the earth, rain and wind, and ripped holes in the sky.

Our science has brought pain as well as joy; our comfort is paid for by the suffering of millions.

We are learning from our mistakes, we are mourning our vanished kin, and we now build a new politics of hope.

We respect and uphold the absolute need for clean air, water and soil.

We see that economic activities that benefit the few while shrinking the inheritance of many are wrong. And since environmental degradation erodes biological capital forever, full ecological and social cost must enter all equations of development.

We are one brief generation in the long march of time; the future is not ours to erase.

So where knowledge is limited, we will remember all those who will walk after us, and err on the side of caution.

This We Resolve

All this that we know and believe must now become the foundation of the way we live.

At this turning point in our relationship with Earth, we work for an evolution: from dominance to partnership; from fragmentation to connection; from insecurity, to interdependence.

CHAPTER 4

WHY DO WE UNDERVALUE LIFE?

A friend once joked that whenever he wanted to sell his car, the dealers offered him a paltry price; and whenever he considered buying a second hand car, the price they quoted to him was astronomical. "It is always a buyer's market when I wish to sell," he laughed.

Indeed, we are very particular that we are not cheated or defrauded in our business transactions. We do not like to be made fools of. We take care to ensure that nobody takes us for a ride.

And yet, we are ever ready to underrate ourselves and our life!

"I am no good; I can never be successful."

"Life is so difficult, it's not worth living."

"I am utterly weary of this life and I don't care to live anymore."

"I cannot cope."

"I cannot manage."

"I'm losing control."

WHY DO WE UNDERVALUE LIFE?

Do you know how often people say these words to me?

Why would anyone want to throw away their lives? How could anyone grow tired of living?

When you were a little baby, your parents and family doted on you! They were thrilled when you took your first steps; they were elated when you uttered the first words, and they rushed to obey your every command when you ordered them to do this or that.

But you know you were not always so angelic. Sometimes, you cried non-stop, all night; sometimes you threw up all that you had eaten; sometimes you lay there, ill and feverish, barely opening your eyes.

Your parents did not complain. They did not say they were weary and exhausted and had had enough of you. They held you close; they comforted you; they hugged and kissed you to make you feel better. They took the best care of you.

Why can't you extend the same loving care to yourself? Why don't you realise that you are precious – and that your life is your most valuable possession?

Why do young people give up so easily? There are several reasons for this:

1. Sometimes, teenagers tend to feel 'trapped' by situations they cannot handle. They find it impossible to deal effectively with a crisis. They feel that they cannot get help or relief from any quarter. At such times, they feel that a quick 'escape' is the best option open to them.

   But the truth is, you don't have to feel so helpless, hopeless and lost! Surely, there are people you can talk to – and believe me, even confiding in another can lower your stress levels. Unfortunately, children tend to turn away from their parents at such times, although this is a mistake. It is not that your parents don't understand you; it is just that they may

WHY DO WE UNDERVALUE LIFE?

not in their wildest dreams imagine that you are taking things so grimly!

In any case, if you feel you cannot talk to your parents, choose your favourite aunts / uncles; unburden yourself to your friends; seek the guidance of your elders / teachers. But stay connected! The best antidote to stress is simple conversation – sharing your thoughts with another!

2. Some teenagers feel a sense of rejection and alienation; they feel unwanted and unloved – and while many of us tend to feel this way occasionally, teenagers are sometimes overwhelmed by this thought that nobody cares for them.

This, of course, is not true! When young people are having a good time, they don't remember to call up their parents or even attend to their responsibilities at home. But this does not mean that you are neglecting your parents, does it? So too, you must realise that when you fail to connect with your parents and do not share your anxieties and fears with them, they may not be aware of the real situation.

Your family and friends will never reject you — and you must get rid of the feeling that you are being rejected, which is only the result of your own pessimism and negative thinking.

3. May be, you are guilty or ashamed of something? All of us pass through such emotions — you are not the only one! Everyone has failed a maths test at one time or another. Almost everyone has been punished for some wrongdoing in school. Everyone has quarreled with their close friends and 'stopped talking' to them; and I am afraid many impressionable young school students have imagined that they are in love, and felt 'rejected' when their advances are rudely turned down!

These are phases, stages of everyone's growing-up years, and the important thing to do in such situations is to realise that such feelings are only temporary. In the long-term perspective, they will seem trivial and petty when you look back on them after five or ten years.

I realise that some young people may have got themselves into 'serious' trouble – stealing, substance abuse or committing petty crimes. In such cases, you do need to feel ashamed and guilty! But don't just stop there. Shame and guilt can be wiped out if you make the appropriate reparations. So, deal with your guilt positively: a) confess to your parents; b) apologise to them; c) seek their help to repair the damage caused. It's simple when you handle it one step at a time! When you seek to remedy a bad or even a desperate situation, you will find that even the smallest step, the least initiative will help to ease your guilt – and make you feel a whole lot better!

4. Low self esteem – not really liking yourself – is a common problem with teenagers. "I wish I were fairer"; "I've got to lose some weight"; "How I wish I were taller"; "If only my nose

was not so sharp", are oft-felt unkindnesses to one's own self.

My suggestion to these youngsters is: focus on your strengths, *not* your weaknesses! Dwell lovingly on what you *have* rather than moan obsessively over what you do not have!

I do not know how often I have heard young people refer to themselves in unkind terms – such as 'dumb', 'stupid', 'clumsy' and so on. Do not put yourself down! Do not be rude, and unkind to yourself! If you do not love yourself,

> DIFFICULT TIMES HAVE HELPED ME TO UNDERSTAND BETTER THAN BEFORE, HOW INFINITELY RICH AND BEAUTIFUL LIFE IS IN EVERY WAY, AND THAT SO MANY THINGS THAT ONE GOES WORRYING ABOUT ARE OF NO IMPORTANCE WHATSOEVER...
>
> ISAK DINESEN

WHY DO WE UNDERVALUE LIFE?

if you are not kind to yourself, how can you expect others to love you and be kind to you? And, let me beg of you, dear youngsters, don't aspire to 'look' or 'be' like the models and film stars whom you admire! How dull and boring the world would be if we were all uniformly tall, slim, fair, perfect-looking specimens like "drawing room" displays! If at all you need role-models, choose great examples: be compassionate like Mother Teresa; be courteous like Queen Elizabeth; be warm and kind like Abraham Lincoln!

5. Peer pressure is another 'thorn in the flesh' for today's youngsters. The obsessive need to 'keep up' with friends, to do all that they do, can be a heavy burden on their psyche. They are constrained to be what they are not; behave in ways which are alien to them; create a false 'image' which suits the 'group' they belong to. Peer pressure must be resisted when it threatens to alienate you. And the remedy to this is — always be yourself!

When all these stress-causing factors mount up together then it is that teenagers begin to undervalue themselves and their lives. They are overwhelmed by negative emotions. They feel that they are failures in life. They are convinced that they must be a source of disappointment to their loved ones; some of them may get into the classic victim syndrome. They fail to see that there can be a way out of the dreadful situation they are in.

Some of them feel, tragically, that ending their life is the only solution to their problems.

> **What do you choose – to 'rank' or to 'link'?**
> Most humans are born with two basic social-emotional modes, 'ranking' and 'linking'. We are ranking when we focus on status/power/influence—comparing ourselves with others. We are linking when we focus on liking/loving/living in harmony and peace with others. The two are somewhat mutually exclusive, in that if you focus on one, the other melts away. Sadly and ironically, the people who really want and need love the most have grown up in an environment that focused on 'ranking', so they focus on it too, rather than on 'linking'.
> *Elaine N. Aaron*

CHAPTER 5

OVERCOMING DEPRESSION

Depression can be a serious setback for youngsters. True, many adults also suffer from depression — but their coping mechanisms are better, as also is their capacity for mature response and reaction to stress.

When young people are depressed, they tend to focus on all their negativities — their failures, their weaknesses, their disappointments and guilt. Depression disables their mental make-up so that they are unable to see the positive side of things. As for recognising their own worth, their merits and their capabilities — they dismiss the very thought that they have such traits at all! In short they are led to believe that things will never ever go well for them, ever again!

The possibility of being happy, of laughing, being successful and content — all of this is utterly discounted, in their unhappy mental condition.

Depression must be fought even as we fight an infection or attack. It incapacitates us so that we are unable to think clearly and solve problems decisively.

The unfortunate thing is that the more we succumb to depression, the more distorted our thought and perception becomes, so much so, we fail to realise that it is not really the situation which is so bad, but our depression which makes us think so. In fact, mole hills appear to be mountains; problems seem insoluble; and it appears that there is no one, nothing that we can turn to!

> DEPRESSION IS A PRISON WHERE YOU ARE BOTH THE SUFFERING PRISONER AND THE CRUEL JAILER.
>
> DOROTHY ROWE

But such depression can be fought, conquered and cured with just a little effort. All we need to do is:

1. Open up to friends / family / elders.
2. Connect with people whom we love and trust.
3. Avoid the company of negative, pessimistic people who aggravate our depression.
4. Seek counseling and guidance.
5. Avoid isolation and solitude by seeking the company of happy, pleasant people, or taking up some form of exercise, physical or creative activity.
6. Adopt a healthy diet, as junk food can negatively impact your mood.

One thing we must avoid: harbouring the thought of escape – or giving up on life!

How to Conquer Depression

- Do not set difficult goals for yourself, or take on additional responsibilities which you cannot handle.
- Break large tasks into small ones, set some priorities, and do what you can as and when you can.
- Do not expect too much from yourself too soon, as this will only increase your feelings of failure.
- Try to be with other people; it is usually better than being alone.
- Force yourself to participate in activities that may make you feel better.
- Try engaging in mild exercise, going to a movie, a ball-game, or participating in religious or social activities.
- Don't overdo it or get upset if your mood is not greatly improved right away. Feeling better takes time.
- Do not make major life decisions such as changing jobs, getting married or divorced, without consulting others who know you well and who have a more objective view of your situation. In any case, it is advisable to postpone important decisions until your depression has lifted.

- Do not expect to snap out of your depression. People rarely do. Help yourself as much as you can, and do not blame yourself for not being up to par.
- Remember, do not accept your negative thinking as permanent. It is part of the depression and will disappear as your depression responds to treatment.
- If need arises, do not hesitate to seek help from a professional counsellor. No matter how much you want to beat it yourself, a psychologist can help you recover faster.

Courtesy: Donald J. Franklin, Ph.D.

CHAPTER 6

SUICIDE IS NOT A SOLUTION!

I was once asked this question at a youth gathering: what do you think of the people who end their own life: are they very, very brave – or are they just cowards?

I replied that it was not courage or cowardice that made people attempt to end their own life. Rather, it was a result of a momentary insanity – a moment when these people felt that they had no one to turn to; that no one, nothing could help them out of their despair.

I called it momentary insanity because their belief is patently false! How can anybody imagine that no power in the world can help them? How could they presume that their condition is so dire and difficult and that the rest of the world is happy and peaceful?

I am not talking about 'heroes' and 'legends'; but there are millions upon millions of men, women and children for whom daily life is a struggle. They survive against all odds; they face challenges with fortitude. Should we not consider the plight of those who are far worse off than we are?

SUICIDE IS NOT A SOLUTION!

- Have you failed an exam? Think of youngsters who cannot afford their education.
- Have you been punished by your parents or teachers? Think of the countless orphans who live on the pavements and railway platforms.
- Have you been unsuccessful in a competition or an entrance test? Think of youngsters who are badly beaten up and tortured by the police.
- Do you feel unwanted or unloved? For a change, why don't you try to love and care for others?

> OH, YOU WEAK, BEAUTIFUL PEOPLE WHO GIVE UP WITH SUCH GRACE. WHAT YOU NEED IS SOMEONE TO TAKE HOLD OF YOU — GENTLY, WITH LOVE, AND HAND YOUR LIFE BACK TO YOU.
>
> TENNESSEE WILLIAMS

The important thing is that you must not let depression lead you to suicidal thoughts: for suicide is not an option.

I am a Hindu; but I respect and revere all religions of the world – and believe me when I say, that all of them condemn suicide as vehemently as murder!

Suicide is not a solution to any of our problems. In fact it only worsens our condition and will prolong our agony after death – and in the lives to come!

The fact of the matter is that we do not have the right to take away what we cannot give. We cannot give life; how then can we take it away, even from ourselves?

They tell me that there was a thought provoking play staged at London's West End, on a man's right to euthanasia or mercy killing. The title of the play was a challenging question: *"Whose life is it anyway?"*

I can give you the answer to that question: it is God's life – not yours or mine! As long as we wish to live here on God's good earth, it is of course our life; we can do as we please with it. But life is an asset entrusted to us for safe keeping. We cannot throw it away; and we do NOT have the right to bring it to an end!

My young friends, do not make the mistake of imagining that suicide is heroic, and that it will make people admire you or look up to you or feel sorry for you.

Do not imagine either that you are 'punishing' your parents or friends or teachers by taking away your own life. You are punishing yourself!

Don't be deceived into thinking that suicide is an escape, a solution, or an end to your misery: It is the worst sin against the self and the spirit and God who created you.

> Suicide is not a solution, it is an end before a solution can be found. It cannot be considered an option, for an option denotes we have a choice, and death robs us of both option and choice. Death is an irreversible act that does not end the pain, for it remains in those who are left behind. Even people who are totally alone, and take their own lives, transfer their pain to those of us in society who do care, and we do – care!
>
> *Stephen L. Bernhardt*

CHAPTER 7

PRACTICAL SUGGESTIONS

How can you make friends with life? How can you make the most of your life and claim your rightful share of joy and peace?

Let me offer you some practical suggestions in the pages that follow. But do remember that these are not merely for reading; they are meant to be put into practice!

PRACTICAL SUGGESSTIONS

1. Take Care Of Your Thoughts

I always say to my friends: thoughts are things; thoughts are forces; thoughts have the power to make or mar your life. Therefore, take care of your thoughts!

Many of us are dismissive about our thoughts. "It is only a thought," we say to ourselves. "Nobody can see it or feel it; it is hidden in the deep recesses of my own mind."

> You are today where your thoughts have brought you; you will be tomorrow where your thoughts take you.
>
> James Allen

It may be that others cannot 'read' your mind. But your thoughts will influence your actions and words; your actions will shape your character; and character is destiny. So, if you are not careful, your thoughts will affect your destiny.

If your thoughts are positive, optimistic, good, wholesome – so much the better for you. If, on the other hand, they are negative, pessimistic, suicidal thoughts – they will only lead to your ruin and destruction.

Therefore, I say again and again: change your thinking and you will change your life!

> NURTURE YOUR MIND WITH GREAT THOUGHTS; TO BELIEVE IN THE HEROIC MAKES HEROES.
>
> **BENJAMIN DISRAELI**

2. BE BRAVE!

Rightly has it been said: cowards die many deaths, but the brave live their lives fully!

The important message of the Gita is: "Stand up and fight!" Zoroaster too, tells us, "Fight ceaselessly with evil." Jesus had to fight Satan. Buddha had to fight Mara. They fought bravely, and they conquered the self.

The message of all religions is: be brave! Be courageous! Life is a battlefield of values – and

> COURAGE IS DOING WHAT YOU'RE AFRAID TO DO. THERE CAN BE NO COURAGE UNLESS YOU'RE SCARED.
>
> EDWARD VERNON RICKENBACKER

each one of us must stand up and be counted on the side of whatever is good and righteous.

Often problems seem to haunt us, making our daily life difficult and unbearable. It is only courage that will help us to play the game of life.

If you have taken part in an obstacle race, you will know this: the greater the number of hurdles you may have to cross, the more interesting the race becomes. So it is with life. The greater the number of challenges we face, the higher the number of difficulties we surmount, the stronger do our spiritual muscles grow. We can face life with a sense of satisfaction and fulfillment. Let us learn to roar like a lion, not bleat like a lamb: instead of longing for the 6-pack abs of the film stars, let us aim to build a spiritual 6-pack that God will appreciate! Let us straighten our spine and stretch out our chest with courage and fortitude and we can see that we will achieve more, much more than our expectations.

3. Link Up With a Higher Source of Power

May I say to each and everyone of you – wherever you may be, whatever your condition, you must never ever feel that you are alone – for One there is, Who is always watching you, watching over you, guiding you, guarding you with the greatest love: God.

Here is my *mantra* for the modern man: you are not alone: God is with you.

God is our loving Father; He is our kind Mother; He is our Friend in light and darkness; He is our Support and Sustenance in hours of crisis and distress. We are His loving children. Why then should we feel afraid? How can we feel lonely, rejected, unwanted, unloved, frustrated or depressed when each one of us is bound to Him with invisible links?

You are not alone: God is with you, now and at all times. You only have to call out to Him, and you will feel His presence. You only have to think of Him, and He is with you, and within you!

Think of a young man who is being sent to a foreign university for his higher education. His father hands him some cash and a plastic card before he leaves the country. The young man reaches his university, settles down in his hostel and starts attending lectures. Soon he runs out of cash...

What the young man does not realise is that his father has given him a credit card which he can use freely, almost anywhere in the world! Whatever he spends, the bill will be paid by his father, whose bank account is safe and secure with money aplenty.

I am sure you will laugh at this foolish young man and think: "How silly! Which century is he living in?"

PRACTICAL SUGGESSTIONS

Similarly, God, the Father of us all, has reposed unlimited 'credit' and hope in us, and has sent us to this earth to fulfill our destiny! And each new day that dawns is a symbol of his abiding hope in us – giving us 'credit' for another chance, another day to fulfill our purpose in this life.

Link up with God – now and always. He is the unfailing source of all that you need – hope, faith, enthusiasm, energy, good health, success, wellbeing, prosperity and all the good things of life.

> WHEN WE CAN'T PIECE TOGETHER THE PUZZLE OF OUR OWN LIVES, REMEMBER THE BEST VIEW OF A PUZZLE IS FROM ABOVE. LET HIM HELP PUT YOU TOGETHER.
>
> AMETHYST SNOW-RIVERS

Link up with God – and you will never feel lost or lonely.

Everyone who is given a credit card for the first time needs to master the simple technique of using it effectively. So too with God's credit: you must get into the habit of linking up with Him, effortlessly, easily and instantly – even quicker than sending a text message on your mobile phones. No keys are needed; no pressure of thumbs or index fingers; the network connection is the best in the universe – it never ever fails. All you need to do is think of Him; call upon Him with love and devotion. He is waiting for you to call Him, to think of Him!

Make this a habit. However busy or 'tied up' you may be, take a couple of minutes every hour or so, to re-establish your link with God. New hope, new energy and positive vibrations will flow into your life.

4. Count Your Blessings!

We live in a 'material world'; we cannot get enough of gadgets, amenities, possessions and comforts.

When we look around us, we fail to see the conditions of those who are worse off than we are – instead we only look at the rich and the powerful, the mighty and the influential, and we yearn so needlessly – "Why can't I be like them?"

Why don't I have a Benz? Why can't I have a bungalow to call my home? Why can't I go abroad for my holidays? Why can't I shop in the best stores for branded products?

> WHEN I STARTED COUNTING MY BLESSINGS, MY WHOLE LIFE TURNED AROUND.
>
> WILLIE NELSON

Tell me, do you ever look at the migrant labourers living on the sidewalks of roads in crowded localities and say to yourself: "I thank God that I have a roof over my head, a home to call my own!" Do you ever cast a glance of compassion at severely disabled people, who are bravely struggling to live a dignified life and say to yourself: "How fortunate I am, that God has given me healthy limbs and good vision and speech and hearing?"

If you are, on the other hand, a differently abled person, have you thanked God for giving you a healthy heart and a good appetite and other faculties?

Count your blessings! The trouble with most of us is that we dwell incessantly on our negatives – on what we don't have, rather than on what we have. And in the bargain, we overlook the most precious gifts that God has bestowed on us in such abundance!

PRACTICAL SUGGESSTIONS

It is not for nothing that Reiki practitioners and others emphasise what they call an 'Attitude of Gratitude' – because saying 'Thank you', and feeling grateful are wonderful ways of infusing yourself with positive energy.

Count your blessings! You are far more fortunate than you think.

Count your blessings – and thank God for the great gifts of life!

> THE HARDEST ARITHMETIC TO MASTER IS THAT WHICH ENABLES US TO COUNT OUR BLESSINGS.
>
> ERIC HOFFER

5. Get Creative!

The word 'leisure' is derived from the Greek word 'leiber' which means free as opposed to slave.

Leisure is associated with free time and the freedom to do what you like with your time — after your legitimate work, your lessons and your duties are attended to.

In my days, young people chose a wide range of joyful, creative activities to fill their leisure time: some of them took up arts, crafts or painting; a few took to music; still others discovered the world of books...

Nowadays, all young people seem to do is watch TV — or sit hunched over a computer screen.

I do realise I cannot wish away satellite TV and computers — but I urge young people not to become slaves to this kind of obsession, which is

PRACTICAL SUGGESSTIONS

fast threatening to become an addiction similar to drug abuse!

Be creative! Discover the special and unique talents God has blessed you with. Learn more about yourself and all that you can achieve without the aid of machines and gadgets.

I must give full credit to our schools and colleges for offering a whole wide range of activities which you can participate in – public

> EVERY DAY IS AN OPPORTUNITY TO BE CREATIVE – THE CANVAS IS YOUR MIND, THE BRUSHES AND COLOURS ARE YOUR THOUGHTS AND FEELINGS, THE PANORAMA IS YOUR STORY, THE COMPLETE PICTURE IS A WORK OF ART CALLED, 'MY LIFE'. BE CAREFUL WHAT YOU PUT ON THE CANVAS OF YOUR MIND TODAY – IT MATTERS.
>
> INNERSPACE

speaking, debates, dancing, singing, group games, quiz, painting, poster making, collage, dramatics, graphical arts – the list is endless!

There is so much more to life than watching the idiot box, as it is so aptly called. Passive TV viewing makes you dull, lethargic and listless. Leave that couch or sofa and discover the open, wide world outside your drawing room! At least take a walk; or go out and breathe the fresh air! Better still, create something new, give expression to your inner life and experience the sparks of your creativity!

> CREATIVE THINKING IS NOT A TALENT. IT IS A SKILL THAT CAN BE LEARNT. IT EMPOWERS PEOPLE BY ADAPTING TO THEIR NATURAL ABILITIES.
>
> EDWARD DE BORO

6. Never Give Up!

It was Winston Churchill who popularised the slogan – Never, never, never give up! Never, never, never give in!

What is the point in going on, if circumstances are so bad, someone asked him: "All the more reason to go on! If you are going through hell, you must keep going!" was his reply.

Many people whom you regard as successful and fortunate, are people who kept going against all odds – Infosys Founder, Narayan Murthy sold his wife's jewels to set up his new venture; Sachin Tendulkar grew up with *mohalla* cricket; J.K. Rowling, the lady who created the phenomenal Harry Potter, faced several rejections and disappointments.

But they never, ever gave up hope. They never, ever, gave up trying!

All of them did not follow the beaten route; they did not take entrance exams, to gain admission to IIT or IIM or MIT.

"All things are possible until they are proved impossible," says Pearl S. Buck, "and even the impossible may only be so, as of now."

I have always been inspired by stories of people who never, ever gave up – and I have shared them with friends who have also found them uplifting and motivating. So here are some specially chosen for you, the readers of this book:

> NEVER GIVE UP, FOR THAT IS JUST THE PLACE AND TIME THAT THE TIDE WILL TURN.
>
> HARRIET BEECHER STOWE

- The great composer Beethoven was often clumsy and awkward with the violin. His teacher referred to him as a "hopeless composer".
- Albert Einstein could not speak properly till he was four, and could not write properly till he was seven. His teacher described him as "mentally slow".
- Louis Pasteur, John Keats and Bill Gates were considered mediocre students.
- *Jonathan Livingston Seagull*, the inspirational bestseller by Richard Bach, was turned down by no less than eighteen publishers before Macmillan finally published it in 1970.
- *Gone With The Wind* was turned down by twenty-five publishers!
- Jack Canfield and Mark Hansen faced rejection at the hands of thirty-three publishers when they brought out the first volume of *Chicken Soup For The Soul*. But they got plenty of insults: "It's too nicey-nice." "Nobody wants to read these short little stories."

- A tour manager said to Elvis Presley: "You are not going anywhere. You ought to go and drive a truck!"

But these brave men and women, never, ever gave up! They pursued their goal with conviction and courage – and they made their dreams come true with their own effort and perseverence.

True, they became 'superstars' in their fields – but they worked very hard to achieve success.

> IT'S NOT THAT I'M SO SMART; IT'S JUST THAT I STAY WITH PROBLEMS LONGER.
>
> ALBERT EINSTEIN

7. Believe And Achieve!

J. K. Rowling, Henry Ford, Bill Gates, Richard Bach, Soichiro Honda – all these people were high achievers who believed in themselves. Mind you, they believed in themselves even when people around them did not believe in them, and that is even more remarkable, isn't it?

If you wish to make the most of your life, if you wish to forge ahead with your dreams and desires, you too must believe in yourself.

Experts tell us that to achieve results, we must not only act, but also dream; we must not only plan and implement, but also believe.

Therefore, believe in yourself. Believe and achieve!

The Bible says: everything is possible to him who believes.

One of the greatest success stories of contemporary business is that of Steve Jobs, co-founder of Apple Inc. This is what he believes:

Your time is limited, so don't waste it living someone else's life. Don't live with dogma – the results of other people's thinking... Have the courage to follow your heart and intuition... everything else is secondary.

> MAN OFTEN BECOMES WHAT HE BELIEVES HIMSELF TO BE. IF I KEEP ON SAYING TO MYSELF THAT I CANNOT DO A CERTAIN THING, IT IS POSSIBLE THAT I MAY END BY REALLY BECOMING INCAPABLE OF DOING IT. ON THE CONTRARY, IF I HAVE THE BELIEF THAT I CAN DO IT, I SHALL SURELY ACQUIRE THE CAPACITY TO DO IT EVEN IF I MAY NOT HAVE IT AT THE BEGINNING.
>
> MAHATMA GANDHI

PRACTICAL SUGGESSTIONS

Believe in yourself – and you will find that others share your beliefs. Remember, do not hesitate to ask others for help and advice. Believe too, in the goodness and understanding of others!

In the Sadhu Vaswani Mission's Medical Complex in Pune, we have a super speciality cancer hospital. We come across some patients who have to undergo both radiation and chemotherapy to check cancer growth. They too, have heard horror stories about the treatment; but we find, time and again, they rise to the challenge. They say to themselves, "I can do it! I can go through this and survive my illness!"

Do you find exams and study deadlines stressful? Don't lose belief in yourself. There are hundreds and hundreds of alternative courses available – some of them, more congenial to your temperament; more suited to your mindset.

Believe in yourself – and pave your own way to success and happiness.

Truly has it been said that we harm others by our deeds, but we also harm ourselves by our negative thoughts and wrong beliefs.

You have been told to love your neighbour as yourself; but let me tell you, at least love and respect yourself as you love and respect others!

> TO DESIRE IS TO OBTAIN; TO ASPIRE IS TO ACHIEVE.
>
> JAMES ALLEN

8. STAY CONNECTED!

If you wish to love every moment of your life, stay connected! Stay connected to God; connect with other people, your fellow human beings; stay connected to your inner self, stay connected to the wonderful world of nature!

At times, many of us are trapped in a painful or bitter situation when we do not want to stay in touch with anyone – not even with God, not with any of our friends.

Do not allow this bitterness and unforgiving attitude to dwell long in your heart: you may or may not be hurting others – but you are most certainly hurting yourself!

Stay connected with people – not only with your friends and loved ones, but also with people at large, people you meet on trains or buses, people you see on the road.

Connecting with other people is important — because you must never lose sight of the fact that you are a part of humanity. You are not an independent, autonomous entity without roots and links. You and others are parts of God's Creation, parts of each other.

When you develop this kind of connectivity, you will stop being obsessed with yourself, your desires, your failures, your disappointments and your personal frustrations.

> THE MOST BASIC AND POWERFUL WAY TO CONNECT TO ANOTHER PERSON IS TO LISTEN. JUST LISTEN. PERHAPS THE MOST IMPORTANT THING WE EVER GIVE EACH OTHER IS OUR ATTENTION.... A LOVING SILENCE OFTEN HAS FAR MORE POWER TO HEAL AND TO CONNECT THAN THE MOST WELL-INTENTIONED WORDS.
>
> RACHEL NAOMI REMEN

PRACTICAL SUGGESSTIONS

You need to come out of the shell of self-centered thinking and become aware of others, become sensitive to others' needs.

When you crack open the shell of selfishness and emerge like the beautiful butterfly from its pupa, the thought will automatically come to you that others need you – the world needs you and the help that you alone can offer.

More often than not, we are so overwhelmed by ourselves and by our own misery and unhappiness that we fail to perceive how we can help make others' lives better!

Staying connected with people means moving out of yourself to give to others – give of your time, efforts and smiles!

Stay connected with nature – or you will lose out on beautiful moments of joy and serenity. Go out into the fresh air and the wide open spaces. Take in the sights and sounds and the scent of nature. Feeling the warm sunshine, feeling the whiff of the fresh rain falling on the parched earth, receiving the gentle touch of the fresh breeze on your face can add lustre to your life.

Stay connected with people – for they and you are part of God's beautiful pattern of creation.

Above all stay connected with God – and you will never, ever feel alone, unloved and unwanted, ever again!

> BEFORE COMPUTERS, TELEPHONE LINES, TELEVISIONS AND MOBILE PHONES CONNECTED US, WE SHARED THE SAME AIR, THE SAME OCEANS, THE SAME MOUNTAINS AND RIVERS. WE WERE ALWAYS CONNECTED.
>
> JULIA LOUIS DREFUS

CHAPTER 8

A Simple Meditation to Build Positive Thinking and Self Esteem

This is a simple step meditation/reflection which will help you focus on your strengths, and help you build your self esteem. It will also teach you to value the gift of life and love the experience of living.

Step 1: Sit down comfortably. If you are used to meditation, you can take on the posture of *Sukha Asana*; or you can sit on a chair with a straight back, feet firmly placed on the ground, and hands resting gently on your knees.

Step 2: Now close your eyes; take a deep breath. Inhale slowly and deeply, till you feel your abdomen and diaphragm expanding. Breathe out slowly; exhale through your nostrils and if necessary, through your mouth to ensure that your lungs have released all the carbon dioxide.

Breathe in – and breathe out. Repeat four to five times, till you feel completely relaxed.

Step 3: Feel the breath entering and leaving your body. Be aware of your breath as a lifeforce – vital, positive, infusing you with new life and new energy every time you breathe. As you inhale, feel your connection with the Universe which sustains you and surrounds you, feel your connection with the five elements; as you fill your lungs with air, be aware that the five elements are also a part of you. Feel your interconnectedness with all that is. Feel your sense of belonging to this Universe.

As you breathe out, throw out all the negative energy building up within you. Empty your consciousness along with your lungs. Empty out all that is getting you down, pulling you down to despair and frustration. Feel lighter; feel that you belong to the Universe.

Step 4: Now begin the process of visualisation.

Option A: (For those who are used to computers).

Create a mental picture of yourself, seated before a monitor. Open the folder MY DOCUMENTS. Open the folder with your name in block letters. Imagine the word files stored in the folder: ENTER one after another – Confidence, Enthusiasm, Positive Thinking,

Energy, Love, Friendship, Success, Achievement, Growth, Maturity, Wisdom, Peace, Prosperity...

Your personal folder is being filled with all the positives of life. Go over the folder – and feel good about yourself!

Next – visualise the list of negatives that come up before you – diffidence, discouragement, disappointment, frustration, lack of opportunity, failures and so on...

As each negative flashes on the monitor, select and DELETE each one so that it disappears from your screen – and your personality. DELETE each negative firmly and deliberately.

> MEDITATION IS NOT TO ESCAPE FROM SOCIETY, BUT TO COME BACK TO OURSELVES AND SEE WHAT IS GOING ON.
>
> THICH NHAT HANH

A SIMPLE MEDITATION TO BUILD POSITIVE THINKING ...

Now, your personal folder is free of all negatives and overflowing with positives. Internalise the positives in the CPU of the mind. Feel your own sense of self worth and self esteem. You are a wonderful and unique being – and you can write your own success story!

Option B: (For those who are not familiar with computers).

Visualise yourself seated at an executive table. Before you is an **IN** TRAY. It is full of envelopes addressed to you. Each one has a label: Confidence, Enthusiasm, Positive Thinking, Energy, Love, Friendship, Success, Achievement, Growth, Maturity, Wisdom, Peace, Prosperity...

Your **IN** Tray is full of all the positives of life. Visualise yourself opening each envelope carefully, and filing away their precious contents in your personal folder. Your folder is now full of all the good things of life.

Next, visualise yourself turning to another tray— marked FOR DISPOSAL. In this tray are piled up all the negatives that you really do not need. Pick up each one carefully – visualise each negative as an old, frayed paper or letter – look at what it contains, and then, firmly and deliberately, tear up each paper – tear it into tiny bits – and put the torn pieces in the waste paper basket under your table: diffidence, discouragement, disappointment, frustration, lack of opportunity, failure and so on…

Now, your personal folder is free of all the negatives and overflowing with the positives. Feel your sense of self worth and self esteem. Realise that you are a wonderful and unique human being who can write his/her own success story!

Step 5: Hold the visualisation of your self worth and self esteem till it is completely internalised. Feel the positive vibrations around you. Hold the picture of yourself as a positive, energetic, vibrant, vital person. You are unique and valuable – and you are the architect of your own destiny.

Step 6: Rub the palms of your hands together and place them gently on your eyes. Open your eyes slowly and see yourself filled with light and fragrance, full of positive energy!